W9-BWI-303

Mesopotamia

The Wesleyan Poetry Program: Volume 78

MESOPOTAMIA

BY

Stephen Tapscott

Wesleyan University Press

Middletown, Connecticut

MIDDLEBURY COLLEGE LIBRARY

9/1975
Am. Lit. Cont.

Copyright © 1973, 1974, 1975 by Stephen Tapscott

Acknowledgement is gratefully made to the following periodicals, in
the pages of which some of the poems in this book were first published:
*Apple, The Carolina Quarterly, The Dragonfly, Epoch, Measure,
Pebble, The Penny Dreadful, Prism International* and *Road Apple
Review.*

PS
3570
A57
M4

Library of Congress Cataloging in Publication Data

Tapscott, Stephen, 1948–
    Mesopotamia.
    (The Wesleyan poetry program: v. 78)
    I. Title.
PS3570.A57M4   811'.5'4   75–11617
ISBN 0-8195-2078-0
ISBN 0-8195-1078-5   pbk.

Manufactured in the United States of America
First edition

For Susan

Contents

Mesopotamia

"... this Communion, this touching on one another of the two rivers, Euphrates and Tigris ... and the enclosing of the land of Mesopotamia, where Paradise was, or the Park of Eden, where man had his beginning: this is marriage, this circuit of the two rivers, this communion of the two blood-streams, this and nothing else, as all the religions know."

—D. H. Lawrence

"David Garrick tells of the power of George Whitefield's voice, that he could make men either laugh or cry by pronouncing the word 'Mesopotamia.'   A story goes that an old woman told her pastor that she often found great support in that comfortable word, Mesopotamia."

—Francis Jacox

Dedications

after an aphorism of Rory Holscher

Blessed
are the fussy, their foreheads
are plowed fields.
Blessed
are the awful,
they scratch their heads bald.
Their noses have no callus.

Blessed are the violent,
they are god's teeth.

& blessed the fat,   they float
inside themselves
noiseless as embryos.
blessed are those who squint
from inspecting the sun.

Blessed are the awkward of heart,
who exaggerate in good faith;
the monstrous who prove the true,
they will inherit
whatever is left.

& blessed, especially
blessed
are the bewildered,
for they have heard all the gods at once.

Afterglow

Maybe the machines have won
after all.
Maybe the moon is not
the one track left
by the herds, vast as doubt, that grazed
across the high prairies & left
only this hoofprint
that fills with poisoned water
unbearably
slowly.

Then what are these tiny hooves where my fingers end?
What is this moon that rises so shyly in my thumb?
What is this
afterglow?

October, a chill

Mist.
It's become October,
a chill
palpable & seamless as grass.
Farther than I can walk to keep
up with the drift,
loose clumps of geese
gather in wedges overhead & pass
on, dissolving southward.

Along the ridge a steady rain
of leaves,

their long vagrant fall
cut short by the swell of the hill.
The aspens are soaked.
The earth smells sour.

In this season I am
haunted by the sense of coal.
Under pressure,
its broad particular stress into
seams,   its slow
consolidation.

My breath abuts the wind &
coheres.   It's that cold.

Underfoot the leaves seethe
as they unravel
but I'm in no hurry.
I tromp home heavy-footed,   over drifts,
through the aspen grove,
like a thin man
planting diamonds.

Mass of the Catecumens

*"In the early Christian church, the Catecu-
mens were Christians by belief who had not
yet been baptised; they were allowed to stay
through the readings and the profession of
faith during the Mass, but they could not
communicate nor remain for the 'Mass of
the Faithful'."*

— *Gaston Lefebre*

I

Askew, on the hill's lean, the honey
locust takes the long light
obliquely.   leaf-fronds that wobble
like a baby's teeth.
          budging.   displaced.

Behind me a migrant shrike
pounds in the scrub.
He too
is too late, usually,
          he never migrates,

he stays
all winter
with his hooked beak
never saying his name.
          mouth that eats & moves on.

The day drops,
westering,
& I
am stuck against sharp edges,
          light ragged as glass.

2

This insistence is not of stones.
The stones graze the hill soporifically,
blind sheep.
This is deeper, this pause.   it is nothing
like sleep.   Though it is late
September here, strands of heat lightning
shimmy over the galloping hills —
details.   details.   I am spread
too thin.   I know & do not avoid
where the loggerheads nest,   where
the fence is broken,   where the shrike
stern with hunger pins the fieldmouse
on the locust thorns & drills its belly
for the pink meat & leaves
the ears,   the snout,   the splayed paws
in an attitude of dumb beseeching.

3

Late September & the honey
locust nurses
the light like a witness
with a grudge.   sullen old
thornpole,   it broods
& waits to remind me,   it says

of course we are immortal.   but
in the meantime we're not getting any
younger.   &
what shall we do, for
pity's sake,
in the meantime?

4

There are moments,   details.   I remember suddenly the
long impatient twist up the spiral staircase in *The Bride of
Frankenstein*. The scientist's assistant is climbing the cas-
tle's highest tower in the storm. It takes so long; he is so
hunched.   One foot, the other.   He is climbing the sum-
mit to trip the switch to capture the lightning-bolt to chan-
nel the energy to fill the cadaver to make life.   Jesus, this
is excruciating.   One foot, the other. He limps determinate
& sterile as a mule.   Chuckling in broken Transylvanian,
he never says his name.   Halfway up the staircase, the hu-
man happens; he hesitates, stoops over slowly to pull up his
stocking: he is alive; he too is involved; you could say
on that landing he is forgiven.

5

the shrike does

what it does

the locust hovers

like a flock of tremblefish

my eyes that never see each other

focus far

6

Dusk slides like an eyelid down.

I am chock-full of details

& reluctant light.   Heading back

toward our rented house,

where my wife is already

waiting for me, I am late already,

my socks dropped down around my ankles in

my sudden hurry to be there.

The Dock

Because I've never liked to swim
I feel at home on the dock.
Plank by plank, I step out
over the radius of the pond
to the end of my tether.
It's my extension,
solid as heartwood.

I've been down enough to the bottom
of water, watched the mud-turtles
slide snout-first
& flutter on the silt floor;
clenched my lungs & investigated
the secretive traffic of fish.
It's all right.
The light there is greenish.

But on a clear afternoon
when the land's so hot
the sky clots
in clouds & the aspens thrive,
pouring out oxygen,
& the pond-dapple cracks the sun &
multiplies it, answering the hard-bright sky,
then I'm glad
enough to walk out over the water
& to spend my time here speculating
on the surface of things.

A Scruple

Just now the problem is
what to do
about the loose-jointed lofty old
outhouse behind the toolshed there
that is so long past its peak.

Whether to do
a job on it,   plug
the shaft,   level & drench
the stoop with kerosene,   strike
a match   & leave
the whole pile blazing once & for all?
Or to dilate its significance?
Endure its endurance?
Plant morning-glories on the scaffold?

There are several schools
of thought.

              & the frame tilts
flimsily,   planks soft as cheese,
& the mudwall hold below
it looms like a hazard,
chock-full & heady
in a hot spell.   I admit.

But there it is.

& the problem remains
essentially a newcomer's scruple
of interpretation.   I know
what the damned thing is there for.
but that's just not enough.

A Corpus

for James Merod

These pilings that describe
my neighbor's field
of trefoil,   their stones
askew—

they aren't, surely, fences.
Their heapishness is pointless.
that's the point.
If I see

in them configurations,
ruined cathedrals,   the
random high-clumped dead,
why then

that's my whiffle.
Here, in the long 5:00
light of eloquent October,
the rocks

quiesce & sprawl.   I
know that,   I admit
them: not, surely,
fences but

a slow crust,   &
where they are is   (to
circumscribe)   where
they aren't.

not to jimmy a steel plow
or turn a horse's leg
or stumble an earnest row
of seeding,

these holes were dug
& hauled & heaped here
in open spills that rubble the margin.
Not, surely, a theoretical

boundary for a spread
of hay—but room for the greening.
These are the loamed-high,
months of

afternoon work for the
long-shuffled dead,   their stones,
where they aren't.
& where I,

random & late as fall
rains, signal & reap them,   in their
order far more tenuous,   & harder,
than crops.

Fat

Once again,
like the grainy native fisherman
repairing his nets,
I spread myself across the hall mirror.
It's too much.

The ambitious thighs,   the bulge
below my chest,
overstated
like the map of Greenland.
I have trusted my imperialistic
tongue far too long.
Now I have to eat
my words:

more is less.

With a patience so distant it is almost guilty
I remember my old
clothes, folded
like the heretic's vestments
in the categories of my dresser.

Nothing fits any more.

The Laundromat

I strip & shiver,
formless with fat.

First the wash,   the whisper & spume
of soapsuds like crazy grace.
It's like stuffing our underwear
into confessionals.

Later I watch the drier,   its
porthole.   On the far side our clothes
dance together, radiant
as they have always aspired,
perfectly-shaped.
Up they flap, ballooning—
the great undersea birds
new-hatched from the year's one egg—

& drag their pockets absently across the damp
heat there that is lighter
than bodies.

Nuts & Berries

Most of the time the assumptions
are simply
too diffuse to sustain
a great weight.

Like the night you were lost so
obscurely in the blue woods,
do you remember?   when
each step tended
in another direction,   each arbitrary;
when you watched the huge
evening stumble through the tree trunks.

You could see your own breath.

You felt
the concern in your belly pucker
like the brain of a walnut.
You could see your own breath
dissolve.   You didn't watch.
        It was tight

but the black
raspberries tasted surprisingly
sweet.
        You survived.

Gloxinia

they all died
off, those pink

gloxinia
in the pot you left

by the north
window,   but

I just kept on
watering them & yesterday

something
else

pointed itself through
where they had been

buried that has
leaves & a nodule a lot

like pink
gloxinia,

as it happens

Laminations

The respectable dark insouciance
of old mahogany.
felled in the rainforest,   planked
in a foreign harbor,
lathed stained & joined
in Boston or Vermont—
where every kind of wood grows
but the mahogany—
in its wide veneer the signature
of the love of America
for the unnecessary.

Therefore American mahogany,
its wild grain stained somber,
lasts
& struts the hollowness of old boxes,
drawers,
cantilevered desk nooks;
anywhere we hide
those scraps & fillips & ribbons
we hoard because they are useless
& inexplicable
& much too important to throw away.

2

And they came & found maple
stands,   & plenty of it.
And it served.
In time they called it by name,
called it moosewood,
sugartree,
hardrock.   And it answered

2 5

by standing firmer,
wood so tough it busts nails.

Therefore we have known maple
all of our lives here,
and it serves:
the seats & rungs of simple chairs,
the breakfast table.
Wood so steady,   it holds up
all that passes
unnoticed through the house,
the meals,   the talk,
all the familiar
hand-me-down
sadness of families.

3

The oak tree dies
so gorgeously
you're glad to see it go.
The notched leaves flush & scatter,
the corns plok,
& even the marrowwood
shuts down
for the season,   leaving the lag
attested in the sheath of rings
& in the trim
& extrovert figures of oak lumber.

Therefore oak beams take their places
responsibly in church pews,
cradles,
beds, floors, &
caskets,   where the bland grain
greets us with ceremony
& recites its lesson to the end:

that those who go down
flamboyantly enough
will surely rise again.

4

Though they are prim, the softwoods,
& fractioned out as lodgepole,
larch & scrubby juniper,
cedars, spruces, & firs,
they bend in the wind.
Nothing is so dependable
as that green,
that Byzantine
untranslatable
monotony.

Therefore pine accepts
alteration with a smooth face.   The pith
of a pine board, sheared clean, takes graciously
to stain;   the singular flavor
of any resin washes into pine's wide
democratic pulp
& never leaves.   wood cropped specifically
to be lost again—
in caskets attics & building beams, & in the sturdy
skeletons of hardwood furniture.
like that part of us which bends to survive,
which suffers,
pine adapts,   stiffly gracious
pine supports and,
vulnerable,   stays constantly secret.

5

Before its fall the cherry
tree lifted its raw wood
lightly, saying the end
of the tree is the fruit
is the cherry
& the waxwings came in a frizz
in late May saying yes yes
the end is near
& is edible.

Therefore when the spring unfolds again
& roots grip
firmer   & the air dampens
after dry cold,
the planks on cherry hutches
seem to limber,
pinken slightly   & shine
in their tight pores with the sap
that still flows
amply
though without them.

Imperative

Even though the snow
this morning changes
each tree to some variety
of birch (it is too bright
for words),
even so
those ubiquitous
brown birds smear
everything here with maps of song.
as if some inland ocean
were studded with musical
islands impossible
to reach.
Oh don't
stop now,
(I try to say)
whatever
the concern must be that squeezes
such whoopee loose
it must be at last a question
of going home.

Flipping & singing,   each line
weaves through a nest of air.
What else
could move drudges
like these so furiously
from the necessary
spin but simply
a reassessment of the obvious?
That the ice-drench can drag
on the swell
of a sycamore,   that song
is a function of disputed
territory

& of a power that is passionately
            heard but glimpsed only
     in its passing
     spurs,

            this is remarkable stuff!

Roots

for Leo Lensing

Just after the snow began
we left your house on the far hill
& drive through the corridor of the valley,
heading home.

Tonight we are the first to come this way;
the road blurs into empty fields
as calmly as a sunken river
over the ocean floor.
Inside the car
is as still as the outside,   the same
fitful shifting of particles,   the same
drift over entryways & crossroads.

Susan talks to me gently.
We look back over the evening's landscape,
watching our tracks
chase constantly after us:
my woman loves your woman,   Leo,
& we are friends.
familiar & lonely as two feet.

We earn our way home
through the snow,
we always do.

Each mile,
pieces of the storm
bloom into constellations
briefly on the warm window.

Hinge

After the storm
with its niagara of white
potshots
that spun through the sumac
thicket late
this afternoon,
the woods are negatively charged.
I
head for home,   the wind
bends me crooked as a hinge,
turns my face to

my steps.
I butt the cold between hulking trees.
Stroked by the bright
wind,   each
one
of them is sketched along
the trunk & branches
with a particular veining of snow
as if
the dark meat of the wood should drop
away like shadow.

Blood Orange

My hands, those strange
contraptions,   work on the fruit,
denuding it;   work
beyond control.

The fingers do their stuff
like good soldiers.
I am a citizen,   I watch

the rind
spread
a map of the world.
The pulp has not long to keep to itself.

It is beyond control as I watch
the dig of nails.
The heart has not long to keep its secret

as I watch & shiver
against the wind.
The circle cannot hold
against the wind & fingers long.

So.
So,   my Napoleons.
The heart is invaded & made my own.

& sap comes violet,
wild & tenuous
as it stains the hand.
I feel a faint old stink of orange.

& the seeds do
an unbodied dance
like the tiny bones' dance in their violet bag
before the womb spits them out.

Housewarming

for Tom and Santina Merwin

May your new home guard
& shelter you from adversaries,
aggressors,
antagonists,
assailants,
beseigers, disputants, wranglers, foes,
sharpshooters, fusiliers & dragoonists,
schisms, factions, breaches & feuds,
brawls, loggerheads, sixes & sevens,
bickering, ruptures, squabble, rumpus & squall,
billingsgate, vituperation & brouhaha,
from Donnybrook Fairs, bear gardens, hornets' nests,
hubbub
& tiffs;

from kudzu & fungi
inside & out,
from infection,
decay, sepsis, mange, murrain & psoriasis,
tsetse, gadflies, weevils, termites, & fleas,
from flummery, buncombe, blarney, oil & honey,
backbite, lampoon, slander & abuse,
improbity, perfidy, crooks, blackguards, poltroons,
    culprits & knaves;

from bad faith, turpitude, false hearts,
forked tongues & sticky fingers,
from the phoney,
the faithless, the shameless, the sneaks,
the talkers, the wheedlers, the jealous
of spirit, the unsquare,
the fishy & the venal,
from blunderers, bumblers, louts & duffers,
intriguers, maneuverers, jugglers, Machiavels & foxes;

34

from the muddy of boot
the clammy of palm &
the tractless of eye;

the extravagantly principled
the scrupulous
the unprincipled
the wishy-washy
the undecided
the neutral &
the dull;

from the lives
of the parties;

from single vision & from Newton's sleep;

from taxes debits & guilt-sodden windfalls,
from flashes in pans & all that glitters,
from Jezebels, Babylons, Sybarites & Epicures,
anchorites dervishes & fakirs,
from tipplers visionaries & bootleggers
from Belial Moloch Mammon Azazel Loki
Asmodeus Mephistopheles Loreleis
bugaboos bogies vamps & wraiths
trolls poltergeists banshees & gnomes
from voodoo & spooks of all creeds;

from orthodoxy heresy skepticism & sects,
from freedom
from bondage,
from indecision, vacillation, & rashness,
from Pharisees, priests, scribes, & professional writers,
from idolatry, materialism, & obvious humility,
from confusion;

3 5

from cads, crachouns, fetishists, lazars, proctors, undines,
    yetis & zimb;
from dark gazebos, velvet sofas, sootflues, coalchutes,
    parapets, kiosks &
closed boxes, from slipped philtres, rusty locks,
    portcullises,
loons, hysteriacs, & Gothic novels,
from bottomless jazz, maypoles, corked bottles, pistols,
    & Freud,
from enchiridions & bad translations;

May it safeguard you from piety, philosophers,
sorcery, pitfalls, eddies, voids, & chasms,
undertow, maelstrom, tides & pests,
from snakes in the grass, wolves at the door, bats
in the belfry, bees in the bonnet & coons in the garbage,
from the banality of evil & from literary allusions;

from penalties scourges cudgels truncheons & quirts,
from dunking puddles, pillories, racks, blocks, &
    thumbscrews,
from jail,
from embarrassment,
from madonnas, seraphs, sages, saviours, & walkers on
    the wind,
from hunger,
from too much of a good thing,
from the smoke of costly cigars;

from curses moths cankers fangs
brambles mildew blight foetor & stench,
from jeopardy, hazard, instability & the stormy petrel,
from gathering clouds, the pricking of thumbs,
    handwriting
on the wall, sirens, flares, drums,

alarums & the yellow flag,
from dogs that bite & drawers that stick,
from uninvited animals with teeth;

May you live free of mottos,
tattoos, icons, ice, friezes, & stone,
from eggheads, meatheads, onionheads, skin-
heads, blockheads, hammerheads, razorbacks & foolish
    consistency,
from elegant symmetry, definitions, archetypes &
    approximations;

from pickles, stews, jams, & hot water
thorns knots pricks & pinches
straits, mazes, coils, rubs, & tickles,
from snags, hitches, stumbling-blocks, tethers & snaffles,
from kill-joys, wet blankets, dogs in the manger,
cramps, saddles, & clipped wings,
feet in the mouth, tongues in the cheek, slaps on the back
& worry-warts;

from smooth sailing & murkiness of feeling,
dinginess, meanness, & unrelieved radiance,
from falling objects, groundswell, earthquake, crop
    failure,
& acts of God, water in the basement, niceness of
    solicitude,
ordeals,
fire,

from doctors, lawyers, dentists, plumbers,
politicians, social workers, morticians, unscrupulous
salesmen, census-takers, anonymous callers,
inlaws, underlings, & bosses,
from pushy neighbors,
cozy neighbors,
neighbors that keep goats,

rude neighbors,
noisy neighbors,
pesty neighbors &
the indifferent

& may you be lonely
only seldom

House Music

What though you crackle
like dimestore taffeta,   rinse
knives in the sink,

           A swart moon slides high.
           A coolness locks
           even the clamorous lilies.

prune the bonzai,
spank the rug,   all
Friday afternoon

           The borderguard lapses in his
           station,   easy,   writing his letter
           home with the foreign stamp

homicide flits through every
synapse,   clean & visible as licks
of flame in a sheared oak;

           required.   The she-deer hunches
           elegantly to pizzle
           by the pond,   the day drains off,

I have been here too long
not to know
to beware,   those

           things generative flow
           to their source,   their poise
           verged on beginning,   & I grow

flashing eyes,   that
floating hair.   The breakfast
grease congeals

           strong & pliant,
           feeding
           on your mouth,   half

opaque as it cools.   In passing in
the hall our daydreams slur—
one survives.

                        dead & bright as the moon.

A Recommendation

Of conifers I think I choose
the blue spruce.
It's by far the most
dependable.   fool-

proof.   disposable:
it dies
from the prickles inward,
a lingering, leisurely

implosion
that occupies the spine
& lets the digroots grapple
to the last.   So tidy,

you can bring it in your home
& snip the needles down
like fingernails
as they turn crisp.

Nothing drastic.   no telltale
wilt.   no testimony
of despair.   it keeps its green
for such a long time.

Advent

Now it is nearing New Year's & the pond has stopped
its complex bendings & has risen
to a single pane
& the spruces go

monochromatic in the brittle light.
December fixes to my window
by white wires.   Now
I seldom walk as far as the top

of the nearest hill,
preferring to loiter through the warm house
here all day,   & sleep too long,
it gets dark so blasted early.

2

Lying still is a way of moving
excruciatingly slow.
Few can do it—

the brown
moles that sleep
under the hill, for instance,
persistent,   smelly,   huddled

nose to flank to conserve heat.
their tunnels, like thumbs,
folded under the soil, seep
air to the innerest pocket,   where
the sleepers finish vanishing.

walled in there, warmed by themselves,
the moles in couples nudge

through the ice-
season,   coasting the underlife
till the green heat heaves
them as close to the light as they ever come.

Poem

for John Berryman

They come seldom & roan from out the brush,
paired together.

Their feet have no heels.
They do not carry antlers.

As if embarrassed to be drawn
below the snow-line
by such a thing as salt
they mince clear of small entanglements

& pause
& swell
& drag tongue slowly
over the brinestone
urging the late snow by with their noses.

They could be
hooded monks at vespers
by the psalter   except
they stain the air a little
randy—

& if I had to choose between them
I couldn't.

Nude Descending the Stair

an elegy for Pablo Picasso,
d. April 8, 1973

I

after six nights & days of rain,
    a morning.   the indistinguishable
        falls together,   the rain
            past,   & everywhere colors
                stare frankly from objects

like shipwreck victims
    suddenly aground.   from the matrix
        of a sycamore,   the call of
            the nuthatch,   song with a hinge
                in its evolution,   song that returns

to its origin like the creak
    of a rope swing.   I recognize
        that nestwarble,   tethered to the
            sycamore by a frail rope.
                chickadees

flirt from the underbrush
    but this one's elusive.   eggwary.
        passing quickly but
            changing,   somehow,
                the simple morning.   I look

& look without finding it

2

Because I loved him without knowing
him I read the newspapers
for a week of elegies.
that helps a little.

44

says there he was bandy-legged,
91,   brass-bald & proud of his
chesthair.   that he loved
women—married several, didn't,

several—drank mineral water
frugally,   painted,   traded,
despised Franco & defended France
in his manner.   that he had to be persuaded

out of bed every morning
with promises of survival.
that his bedroom was dark
where he finished.   It's an adequate

composite.   flat photographs,   fact.
4 columns of statement by the school-
masters.   In one picture,
walking by the beach,

he is wearing only tennis shorts
& dark glasses.   there's his chesthair
but the eyes are shaded,
missing persons

　　3

the eyes, distinct,
　　die alone.   though they fold
　　　　in a dark room,   their sheen is the last
　　　　　　to go,   the sight split
　　　　　　　　like a horse's.
　　　　　　　　like a scientist's.
　　　　　　　　like a lover's: close

enough to splinter but
in its sweep the village entirely,
apivot.   the eyes go, still afloat
as they lower their flags.

but one woman
among her reflections,
one
rictus-tongued with the plunging bull,
the torn horses,   under
the sky's bulb.
one
going fumble-stepped & lifting
one child,   her image,   through
the neighborhood of bombs.   a woman
seen familiarly,   tender & specific as boils.

to see the one
among the possible,
that is enough:
to have seen
her for once, whole & especial.
to recognize her too
as she sits
still in a room among the planes
of color, to find her without
seeking.

as today.
as she sits
here with me watching the sixday water
lose itself widely in the common
lake but changing it,
changing it.

The Yellow Sorrel

It's
curious: the
groundcover keeps our
shapes—there where we
lay among the yellow sorrel—
keeps them so much
longer than it
keeps our
heat

Big Boy

Wound up so crabbed
in the middle of April
the vine in the seed
busted loose,
past circumference, & now the whole

tomato plant aspires
only to the horizontal.
I've tried hoisting it up
on a pole but it's reluctant,
each week's growth

hunches its progress
downward, establishing the durable
old curl.   It's risking soil-blight,
root-rot, categorical scissorings
by wild bugs, raccoon-raids,

slugs, fungus, & midday
shade for this unparalleled
expansiveness, & the fruit's
slung low as plover's eggs,
half buried already.

Mayday, mayday

It's happening again.
Tripped up by the year's melt & now
5 days of rain, congregations of earthworms
rise on their shafts of slither

(thinking   (their functions
are, at best, dispersed)   it's
the Flood again,
at long last)   to the open lawn.

where the robin is
there to meet them,
not laughing
exactly   but hungry,   down

to earth,   in his element,   & not
so easily bamboozled by such
uplifting
prognostications.

Several Gravities

several gravities
pull us
severally & we
configurate

the best we can.
standing firm on
next to nothing.
today I watched

a mantis in the chokecherry
scrub fix a transient
swallowtail, scoop it,
sever its axis

& gnaw
for a while
& then resume its praying,
dense & reverent.

I congratulated the mantis.
I missed the swallowtail's spree.
It was, you could say,
polyphonal.

each in his
right, each particularly
necessary.
lub &

dub of a great pulse
that we believe with both
hands, two eyes,
two breasts, our

pair of sexes.
that far-clinging
union we hear
beneath attention,

as when ancient soldiers,
now millennia
dead, beat their swords
against their bright shields

miles from the city's
walls to mark
the rhythm of
their fearful coming.

Poem...

begun by a picture of my mother as a girl in central Kansas,
standing in a yellow dress in a field of flowering soybeans,
   c. 1932

1

Until the admission of Alaska
to the Union,   the geodetic center
of the United States lay near Lebanon,
in Smith County,
Kansas,
at 39° 50′ north latitude
and 90° 35′ west longitude.

It's one of those unconcerned
cockleburr facts
that becomes pertinent for no reason
but its own
central snag,
making its home wherever
the circumstances.

Oh no
I say to nobody
in particular,   the truth
again,

that hitchweed.

2

This is what happens:
the Missouri & the Colorado rivers,
curling generally southward,
make a kind of wedge—
a land-hammock—

of the broad postglacial plateaus
where the cattle graze on spiny
blue-stemmed grasses interminably.
Under those plains the mountains
tamp their roots: crude
petroleum,   coal,   chalk.

I remember the broad-slumping
barbwire fences
that block off the land there
in squares
definitive as stitches in a quilt.
Going slowly,
their poles are as full of decay
as the news in the random letters
I get from the folks who stayed on:

the old write about the weather
& its harvest,
the young have discovered sex
again.

3

Coldwater: the waitress
in the diner on Route 281
with veins like sprigs of onion under taut silk.
The hiway abuts Route 36W
at Smith Center & goes no further north.

Medicine Lodge: the highschool girls
watch their steadies through the summer
afternoon, spread on their backs
knees akimbo
overhauling Chevy stockcars for the ring.

Lebanon: who must have thought
this was the Promised Land?
Mount Jesus: flat as cowflop.

Walking over the hills
where I live now
I think of her skinny in a light dress,
her hair bobbed short, grinning
in the beanfield,   the weeds
as high as her ears.
I carry that picture everywhere
I move these days,
though by now that dress looks
bleary.   Kodak-yellow.
& that field has been picked
& replanted
& picked   again.

4

Thinroot
cockleburr,
little syndicate of thorns,

I was there too.
I guess I am a harvest too,
a sprinkling of weeds like you.

5

I got out a map
of the Great Plains States to look
for the way they had to take
to leave Lebanon,

Kansas, & the map said:
she's gone.   Look someplace
peripheral.
Those who try to find

a woman in the landscape
will wish they had left
the body under-
ground.

6

The townships clump beside the hiway
like clots of nitrogen along a root.
So long, she told the neighbors,

                    leaving,
                    in a light dress, yellow
                    & sleeveless

(The Best Music is What Happens)

Across the sworl of the
valley the wind
scuffs,   alien but
familiar in its sinuations.
a new wind,   stuff

of silence,   a moving that presses
itself so constantly it somersaults,
spilling over
the scrub in a long diphthong.
like new water's press

over rocks,   that froths
so white it recollects the snow
that shot it,   here
the air lifts,   lowly,   recalling its
country & that passing dialect —

the still pocket always
just over the next hill.
it's no song that I know
well but I know the wind
all melody,   there is nothing

so unnatural as that
march,   the constant transient:
all wings,
no head no
arms no face

but a tumultuous forwarding
over the milkweed pinions.
no wonder the wind moves
water, teasing waves till they flap
in aspiration.

my blood flaps once in passing
& is still.
over, the pegged stars.
downvalley a pheasant
rises,

venusian,
from a field of rain-soaked stubble
arching surely from where she is
at home to where
she is still at home.

Near Slaterville Springs, New York

Those of us who would otherwise
forget have to drive
through the loose empty synapses
of small towns on our way

somewhere else.   Passing
a mile a minute,
we catch what we can
from a distance: the one bank,

the wind-soughed bandshell,
the county hospital & consolidated
school.   & always the several
churches,   each aspiring,

near the center.   Through & past
on the main road,   we slow and
accommodate: 60,   45,   to the quiet
wind through the dead center

of things, watching for children
& our own reflections
in street-level windows.   November light.
The corky houses huddle so close,

each cluster
seems to slow us in its lingering.
Always named after somebody dead.
& somehow we never leave—

in each town,   one clapboard
bungalow,   round white years
clumped like radishes,
a new constellation.

Somehow we live through
a life in every town
we pass at thirty.
In those windows I see my wife,

a grey bright woman;
in every niche I watch us
ripening
together,   distinct

& strung together like a wide
wide field of pumpkins.

To the Green Chapel

The common sun wobbles on
its stem,   the month September
sloped by degrees.   where limber orchards
lean along a hill
& the late fruits glint.

as the wave eased
at Pompeii that season
September cooled them in an amber
light, the preoccupied.   stuck
as they had fixed themselves

in living, in flight.   & one watched
homeward,   one hid her mouth
moist against the sudden
stone,   one held coins
in the frieze of his robe as they left,

still
watchful,   guarding the essential
& freighted with its species.
Curled there yet,
cotyledons.

September, a heaviness sinks us
all, who lie
without rooting,
fleeting & constant in the magma
stop.   what we assume

will boggle us,
& in September: the sun on its
stem like a 7-month fetus,

capable of kicking loose but still
unfinished.

2

the city of seeds
strikes tap in
a kernel of dissolution.   one by
one we

ripen &
drop apart.
impulsive.   walled in.
outside   other men   other women

complex as trees.
we are thinner when we lay us
down alone
together,   membranous as never

erect.   the common light
passes through
as through a plane
window on a west room,

lateral & clear.
such passage hyphenates us,
dust to dust,
day to day.

3

*Lotus seeds are believed to remain dormant
longer than any other seeds known;   some are
reported to have sprouted after hundreds
of years in dry storage.—Natural History* magazine

4

Alone, I'm without
program,   distracted

by whatever is passing—
the jay that twits hostilities
invisibly from his tenure in
the branches,   the plane tree
that hangs
open like a wall of windows,
the fixed
sky,   the bright
& obdurate circumference.
So much needs watching,
my sight is divided.
The dark drops distinctly
in flakes,   the snow
darkens.

5

In the depths,   says Rilke
at Viareggio,
all becomes law.

that awful freedom.
the long frost hatching
the acorn husk.

6

& within this waiting penance.
& in penance the withering
of limits.
& solidly in limits the end of waiting.

In the universe of
an apple a seed
is the sun.

7

It is long time now to chart
the distances,   unsnarl

6 3

like the tree in the apple,
all boiling foliage, fruit, &

unarguably pip.   that Odysseus
met the dead in a ditch
beside a road;   that the underworld
where Persephone descends & rules

& rises looms the depth
of a plowed furrow,
& of a piece;
that the land as we go it

is flat
& underwhelming;   we will climb
to that perspective,
lofty as waists,

& manifest the rippling obvious,
no longer the habitual's
static shebang;
rise & fill

8

& leave like Peter & James & John,
go back without pitching our tents.

9

Follow, then,   the day's drift,   a thin
expansiveness
etched clean as the print
of leaves.   Just so,

the corridor of each stem tends us
by a stern & volatile
passage to
the green chapel.

PS
3570
A57
M4

Tapscott, Stephen.
    Mesopotamia.

PS3570 A57 M4
+Mesopotamia / by+Tapscott, Stephe

0 00 02 0210832 0
MIDDLEBURY COLLEGE